PURIFIED IN THE FIRE

Power of Prayer in the Ashes

Dana L. Nicholson, Psy.D.

WESTBOW
P R E S S®
A DIVISION OF THOMAS NELSON
& ZONDERVAN

Scripture quotations are taken from the Holy Bible, New Living Translation, copyright ©1996, 2004, 2015 by Tyndale House Foundation. Used by permission of Tyndale House Publishers, Inc., Carol Stream, Illinois 60188. All rights reserved.

WestBow Press books may be ordered through booksellers or by contacting:

WestBow Press
A Division of Thomas Nelson & Zondervan
1663 Liberty Drive
Bloomington, IN 47403
www.westbowpress.com
1 (866) 928-1240

Because of the dynamic nature of the Internet, any web addresses or links contained in this book may have changed since publication and may no longer be valid. The views expressed in this work are solely those of the author and do not necessarily reflect the views of the publisher, and the publisher hereby disclaims any responsibility for them.

Any people depicted in stock imagery provided by Getty Images are models, and such images are being used for illustrative purposes only. Certain stock imagery © Getty Images.

ISBN: 978-1-9736-5564-0 (sc)
ISBN: 978-1-9736-5563-3 (e)

Library of Congress Control Number: 2019902494

Print information available on the last page.

WestBow Press rev. date: 4/15/2019

DEDICATION

In loving memory of Michael William Mariotti, my little brother, best friend, and most loyal defender. His death inspired me to honor him with my success and commitment to living a life with no regrets and to my fullest potential. I have purposed that his death will bring life to all aspects of my life. He continues to inspire me, and I couldn't be more blessed to have called him my brother and friend.

Purified in the Fire is also dedicated to my parents. Without their support, love, unwavering belief in me, and commitment to encouraging me to always strive to be my best, this book wouldn't have been possible. I am beyond blessed to have parents who not only taught important life principles but also live them out every day. Their commitment, loyalty, integrity, devotion, and refusal to compromise their beliefs has inspired me to become the woman I am today.

To my beautiful children, who have become some of my greatest teachers. I learn something every day from their love of life, their sense of humor, their bravery to try new things, and their hearts to love others. My children have inspired me to love in ways I never thought possible. Being a mother has been the greatest honor of my life, and I am so blessed to be called Gianna and William's mother.

INTRODUCTION

Purified in the Fire was inspired by my seasons of loss, grief, pain, and sorrow. I was taken to valleys so low in my life that I was barely able to see beyond the walls of my darkness. That's when God showed up. And that's when I learned to pray, really pray. Not just an SOS prayer or "please help" prayer, but the type of prayer where I talk to my Creator and hear from Him in ways I couldn't have even imagined possible. I began writing out my prayers as a way of talking through all that was inside of me and getting it out. I knew I had to give expression to what I was feeling and put to words such tumultuous emotions and feelings. That's when everything began to change.

This prayer journal is meant to do just that for you. I created different categories for the various areas of my life. Doing this helped me stay organized and focused on what God was asking me to pray and whom He wanted me to intercede for. This also allowed me to record the dates that my prayers were answered. This was such an amazing realization for me: God heard me! He answered my prayers, not always in my timing or in the way I thought, but He answered them in the most perfect way for me. And my faith was and continues to be strengthened with every answered prayer.

I know you must relate to those situations in life that just seem insurmountable, where you don't know where to turn as you feel you have tried every solution or plan to overcome. You have asked for advice, sought counsel from professionals, or possibly joined a group or Bible study. Whatever method you have employed, you still come up only half full. And God never intended us to be half full. He has promised us a life of joy, peace, and abundant blessing.

The first step to reaching this amazing place is beginning to write your prayers, your petitions, your pain, your hopes, your visions for the future, and your deepest desires. Something amazing happens as you do this.

What was once a thought, worry, fear, or dread in your mind has now come to life on paper. As you begin praying about these things daily, something miraculous happens. You feel a peace, a weight lifted as you have given it to the One who has the power to create mountain-moving change in your life. And you will begin to see those changes occur. Changes that you never imagined possible. Dreams that you had let die. Inner demons that you never thought you could overcome. They all crumble to pieces as you commit with trust your petitions to God.

As I began incorporating scripture and writing scripture verses under my prayers, I saw God move in mighty ways. Praying His Word is a privilege and a discipline that became part of my daily life. I encourage you to do the same as I did. Open the Bible, read what God has to say about whatever you are going through, read through His many promises to you, and start writing them next to your prayers. Then sit and watch. Watch as He does what only He can do. He will make beauty from the ashes of your shattered experiences. He will, with such precision and gentleness, begin putting the broken pieces of your life back together.

If this all seems too good to be true, then I challenge you to give it a try. Begin using this journal, making it a part of your daily routine. Then prepare to be amazed and awestruck. But most of all, prepare to feel the love of God as you have never felt it before. It is my honor to be a part of this journey with you. Praying with power will change your life!

PURIFIED IN THE FIRE:
POWER OF PRAYER IN THE ASHES

For the word of God is alive and powerful. It is sharper than the sharpest two edged sword, cutting between soul and spirit between joint and marrow. It exposes our innermost thoughts and desires.

—Hebrews 4:12

Yes, ask me for anything in My Name and I will do it.

—John 14:14

THE CURTAIN CALL

Every life has a curtain call. We have all been to plays or theatrical performances and seen curtain calls. We applaud the talent of the actors and actresses as they appear to take their final bows. We acknowledge their talent one final time before we exit the theater. It is a chance for the actors to be appreciated and their hard work acknowledged. Their preparation for the performance, time spent, and energy placed in performing all culminates in that moment. It is joyous, it is happy, and it is well deserved.

Life is much like that. We have a set time here on earth to live as we choose. We have the incredible ability to wake up every day and choose how our day will unfold. Ultimately, we cannot choose what will happen to us in the course of that day, but we can choose how we respond. And that is what leads to how our curtain call will unfold. Thoughts are a choice. Choose well.

WHAT DO WE DO WITH JESUS?

This is the most important question you will ever answer. What have you done with Jesus? Because, at the end of the day, you have to do something with Him. His Word declares that truth. And no one can deny that Jesus is the most influential person in the history of the world. Now many will say, "Of course I believe in Jesus. I know He died on the cross." I believe this is the attitude of most. But I make the challenge that there is a clear and distinct difference between knowing that Jesus died on the cross and *living* like Jesus died on the cross for *you*. And what you do with this will make the eternal difference.

In John 14:6 Jesus states, "I am the way, the truth, and the life. No one can come to the Father except through me." This is an incredibly powerful statement. Jesus declares that He is the Way. When we are endeavoring to find somewhere we have never been, we typically use a GPS device to get there. The path is unclear, and our device displays a map and often audibly speaks directions to us. This is who Jesus declares He is in our lives. He is the way to heaven. He is the way to salvation. He is the way during every minute, during every second, of our day. Do you seek His guidance? Do you look for Him to show you the way in your life?

Jesus declares that He is the truth. What is truth? "In the beginning was the Word. The Word was with God, and the Word was God" (John 1:1). Jesus is the incarnate Word of God. He is the source of all truth. Everything comes from and was made by Him. There is nothing else on this earth that is more pure, honest, and true than Jesus Christ.

By saying He is the life, Jesus makes the powerful statement that there is no life without Him. This is demonstrated beautifully in the lives of people who have given their lives to Christ. Their testimonies are an amazing illustration of how God has worked powerfully in the lives of His people. He breathes life into us when we give our life to Him. Life is no longer an uphill struggle. If you look at the lives of people who don't know Jesus, you will see lives riddled with anxiety, depression, anger, fear, or loneliness. Their hearts are aching and barren. The world will inevitably let us down.

Without the solid rock of Christ on which to rely, people cave under the pressure.

Life is full of hardships, pain, trials, and challenges. Not one person will escape this inevitable truth. In fact, the Bible tells us to expect these difficulties. James tells us, "When troubles come your way, consider it an opportunity for great joy. For you know that when your faith is tested, your endurance has a chance to grow. So let it grow, for when your endurance is fully developed, you will be perfect and complete, needing nothing" (James 1:2–4). Now, read this verse to most people and they stare at you wide-eyed and in disbelief. "Really?" they say. "I'm supposed to be joyful when my sister dies? Joyful when my spouse has an affair? Joyful when I lose my job? Joyful when my child begins abusing drugs? Yeah, right." This is where most quit in their understanding of who Christ is and how He wants to help them.

IN THE FIRE

In November of 2008, life as I knew it changed forever. My husband and I were living in North Ridgeville, Ohio, in a beautiful home he had built for us. We were building our new life together with our one-year-old daughter and a baby on the way. I had recently completed my doctoral program and was in the process of studying for the grueling licensing exam. Jeremy worked in sales and traveled a good deal for his job. He was a successful salesman and provided well for our family.

Something was missing for me there because our families lived in the Pittsburgh area. I wanted to raise our children to know their grandparents and see them often. Although not thrilled with the decision, Jeremy agreed to accept a transfer back to Pittsburgh with his job. We placed our home on the market and prayed that it would sell quickly. Jeremy was transferred prior to the sale of our home, so he moved back to live with his father, and my daughter and I remained in Ohio. I continued to study and raise our daughter, very excited about our new life in Pittsburgh.

After I'd passed the exam, we found a rental home, and our daughter and I moved to Pittsburgh around Thanksgiving of 2008. Being five months pregnant made it difficult for me to organize and move into our home. But I was elated to be back home, and I did it with much joy. We had a cute little yard for our daughter to play in, and I was excited to start making new friends and building a new life.

But, after only a week, my world came crashing down. Jeremy returned home from work at his usual time, but something was different. He was unsettled and anxious. He quickly told me he wanted to grab a six-pack of beer and told me he would be right back. A kiss and he was out the door. I played with our daughter and kept dinner warm until he got home to eat it. What should have taken no more than thirty minutes turned into an hour. I began to worry as darkness fell. Two hours had passed. Fearing for his safety, I called the police. Obviously not immune to these types of calls, they showed up at my house and asked me if my husband liked to frequent bars. They asked where he would go. I adamantly denied this possibility and expressed my fear that he had been hurt. They eventually left and told me they would be looking for him.

Anxious and incredibly fearful, I put our daughter to bed and changed my clothes. I was in complete shock and disbelief at the situation I was facing. There was no way Jeremy would lie to me. He never had. He was always doting, respectful, and honest. There was a logical explanation for this. I tried to sleep, but my heart raced as I vigilantly listened for the garage door. I analyzed every sound, hoping and praying it was him coming home with a reasonable explanation. But it wasn't, and he didn't. Night turned into morning. I managed a few hours of sleep.

Now he did eventually come home, accompanied by a wonderful explanation of where he had been. The details escape me after all this time. But it was horribly unfortunate and unavoidable. He was so sorry and said he'd been very worried about me. And I bought it hook, line, and sinker. As time went on, these "unfortunate" incidents became more and more frequent. He would call to let me know he was going to be "half an hour late." This half an hour would stretch until the next day. And as per his usual, a beautiful explanation followed.

In December he delivered the wonderful news that he had decided to quit his job one day. He was tired of traveling and "didn't want to do it anymore." Those words rang in my ears. They evoked both panic and rage at once. I don't remember much other than asking him what he was thinking and how he expected we were going to live. He calmly explained that he simply couldn't take the pressure of traveling and that quitting was his only option. Only option? There went our health insurance and financial support. And lest he forget, we were having a baby in March. And I thought I was panicked before.

He scurried to apply for government assistance and subsidized health insurance. I couldn't believe we were living this way. I was ashamed and embarrassed and started to become very resentful. This was not the life I had signed up for when I married him. And what scared me the most was that he really didn't seem to care that our life was going down the toilet. This seemed acceptable to him. But I fought to be encouraging and assisted him with looking for other jobs.

As my life was spiraling out of control, I managed to preserve the unity of my family to the public eye. I refused to let this horrible secret seep out beyond our four walls. When Jeremy would disappear over the holidays, I would make excuses for him, saying that he had to visit with his family or he had an unavoidable obligation. I felt awful for lying and was worried that I would be found out. But to me that was the better alternative to admitting my life was falling apart, that my "perfect" family wasn't all it appeared.

March approached quickly, and our baby was due. By this time, depression began to set in and I felt an underlying anxiety almost daily. I never knew when a disappearing act would occur, so I was constantly vigilant. It started wearing me down, and our fights became more frequent. I was admitted to the hospital on March 5 and induced that morning. I called Jeremy, and he came quickly. He brought with him the news that he had had a job interview that morning. The job paid next to nothing and offered no health insurance. I had such extreme emotions coursing through me: utter joy and excitement at the birth of my second child, but extreme worry and fear about our future. How in the world would we pay these hospital bills? Jeremy, on the other hand, was completely unaffected.

Will was born at 7:05 that evening, and I was elated to have a boy. Jeremy, apparently concerned with the quality of the hospital food, insisted that he was going to get a pizza. He left almost immediately after Will made his grand appearance. I lay there, staring at my son who was sleeping in the bassinet beside me. I could hardly believe this perfect little boy was mine. I thanked God for the blessing of his life.

That familiar feeling started creeping back. Anxiety swept over me as I realized Jeremy had been gone over an hour. I knew that it wouldn't have taken that long to get pizza. I tried calling his phone, but I knew the drill: my calls always returned unanswered. Or his phone was turned off. That hour turned to hours as the night swept away. When I realized he wasn't coming back, I sobbed at the harsh reality of my life. This was supposed to be one of the happiest days of my life, and it had turned out to be one of the worst. My husband abandoned my son and me on the day of our baby's birth. Does it get much lower than that? I highly doubted it. And I hated myself for being sad when I should have been so happy. I managed to sleep for a few hours, but the anger that brewed didn't allow much rest.

Jeremy showed up the next morning with another elaborate excuse, one that I easily bought because I didn't want to consider the alternative. He looked tired with dark circles under his eyes. He was lethargic and lay on the couch most of the day. My heart was breaking, but I tried to stay positive and energetic. My parents came to visit with our daughter, and as usual, the image of perfect happy family was resumed. No one suspected a thing. My life was a battlefield of destruction wrapped in such a beautiful picture. But pictures fade, and mine was starting to fall apart.

I wish I could say that things improved once our son came home, but that would be yet another lie. They only worsened. And I slowly became someone whom I never thought I would be. I had always been a strong, confident, and driven woman, but this nightmare started eating away at the very core of who I was as a person. I began feeling insecure, wondering what was wrong with me that my husband chose not to come home at night. He denied any foul play each time and covered his tracks well. Up until I started checking his phone records. It was then that the fragmented pieces started coming together.

In usual drug addict style, his phone records were riddled with multiple calls in the wee hours of the morning. He would call incessantly, literally hanging up and calling right back in desperation. When I discovered these records, I knew the truth. It was a truth I couldn't deny, no matter how badly I wanted to. I confronted him with the evidence. I was ready and knew he would confess and then this living nightmare would be over. But somehow he didn't read the way the story was to end. Jeremy denied any foul play and insisted that these were calls to friends or, better yet, that he hadn't made them. It was laughable. But the joke was really on me, because I was the fool who bought it yet again.

I continued to live this way for two more years. Two years of my husband not coming home, saying he was going to pick up our children but then never show up. My belongings started coming up missing. Things would disappear. When I questioned Jeremy, he said he had no idea where they were or, better yet, what I was talking about. I started to think I was going crazy. In fact, I was told that I was crazy many times. I just didn't know anymore. The hole got deeper and deeper, and my life was entangled in lies and deception. Worst of all, I carried this boulder alone. No one knew my precious secret. I guarded it with my life. And I was determined that I was going to fix this before anyone found out.

Jeremy had accepted yet another job and was at a training in Cleveland, Ohio, for a few days. I received a phone call from the police. My husband had never showed up to training that morning. My stomach hit the floor. I couldn't believe what I was hearing. He completely blew off a work training meeting. And his supervisor and the police were calling me. I was so humiliated and embarrassed. And I could only imagine what they thought of me. But by this time I was desperate and deceived that I actually believed that Jeremy might be in danger. My parents were on vacation in Palm Springs. I called them that morning to tell them Jeremy was missing.

My whole family was concerned and worried, although later on they admitted that they hadn't sensed surprise in my voice, almost like this wasn't my first rodeo. Ah, if they only knew I was a pro rider. Jeremy eventually called, explaining that he had admitted himself to a psychiatric unit in Cleveland. He said he was going to "snap" and couldn't take it anymore. He later produced paperwork securing his alibi. Whether the documents were genuine or fraudulent remains to be seen.

Then one morning the proverbial cat came flying out of the bag at full speed. Easter morning, that is. Jeremy always did holidays with style. The night before Easter he pulled a Houdini and was nowhere to be found. We had Easter plans with our friends at Seven Springs, and I decided to go up without him. I will never forget the heartache of having to put on a smile for my children and act like everything was normal. Everything was far from normal, and the house of cards was about to fall. Jeremy eventually called and said that a drug dealer "took his car keys" when he was passed out. Took his keys! And he didn't know where the car was. Those words rang over and over again in my mind. Our car ... he didn't know where it was. How do you not know where your car is? I was filled with rage that a faceless, nameless person was driving *my* car. My anger, at this point, started to debilitate me. I became so focused on the situation that I began to crumble emotionally.

I called the police, and they told me they had to come to my house. I experienced yet another moment of panic because my two young children were home. I quickly called my mother and told her what had happened. She agreed to come get my kids and take them to her house.

After I'd met with the police, they kindly told me they would call when my car was found. And it was found all right. Completely ripped apart and destroyed in one of the projects near Kennywood. I was mortified. I was sick. But apparently I was not mortified or sick enough, because I stayed. And the drama continued.

It took me quite a while, four years to be exact, before I made the decision to divorce Jeremy. As a Christian, I was adamantly against divorce and refused to terminate my marriage. I clung to that with all I had. But eventually my cord had shred. And the very thread that my family was hanging from finally gave way. Family and friends constantly encouraged me to leave him. And their voices got louder and more persistent as time went on.

I prayed constantly. Mainly I prayed that God would heal Jeremy and set him free from the bondage he was in. I ordered books, listened to pastors, went to counseling. I did everything I could do to make sure that Jeremy would change. We talked for hours about what had to change, and he insisted that it would. I just couldn't believe that God wouldn't want my family together. I knew that He had to want us to work out. But as my depression and anxiety deepened, I knew I could not continue. I knew the end had come.

THE REFINING PROCESS

Once I started the process of divorce, I felt an almost instant peace. My horrific nightmare was over, and I was free to live a life void of lies, worry, suspicion, doubt, and instability. As crazy as it sounds, it was one of the best times of my life. I made new friends quickly, and my life became full and rich. When you live a life like I had for so long, you eventually lose yourself to the drama as it begins to suck you in whole. You become so used to denying yourself that you don't even know who you are anymore. It has been such a wonderful journey getting to know who Dana is and who God created her to be.

1. Rejoicing in Trials

So my story brings me back to what James beautifully articulates about "rejoicing in trials and hardships." I believe I can safely say that what I endured can definitely be considered a trial. Most certainly a hardship. To me, it was downright brutal. I remember being on my hands and knees many a night, crying out to God. I would ask Him where He was. I would ask Him why He wasn't making this better, why He wasn't changing Jeremy when I knew He could. I had faith. I believed. Why wasn't it happening? I was a committed wife. I supported Jeremy. And I thought

I was being "noble" by staying in my marriage when most others would have walked away. I thought I was honoring God through this marriage, but I was really setting myself up to be abused and mistreated and, worst of all, enabling Jeremy. I now know that I played a vital role in prolonging Jeremy's healing and recovery. My tolerance of his despicable behavior allowed him to continue to function as a manipulator, liar, addict, and thief.

Now, I have to be honest. I didn't start out "rejoicing" that my life was going to hell in a handbasket. In fact, rejoicing was the farthest thing from my mind. I was angry, bitter, and resentful. Now I realize I also had a spirit of entitlement. I had the audacity to believe that I "deserved" better than to have to go through all of that, that somehow the pains and misery of life should pass me by. Those things happened to other people, I thought. As my life starting falling apart, my number one priority was making it look like my life *wasn't* falling apart. Around family, Jeremy and I played the charade, acting like all was well. And I believe that in his mind, it was. When I would be out with friends or at my church group, I wore a smile that would light up the room, a smile that illuminated joy, when inside my heart was breaking in two. Maybe I'd missed my calling as an actress, because I played that role well.

Behind closed doors I allowed myself to be the broken, crushed, heartbroken, self that I really was becoming. For four long years, life made absolutely no sense to me. I hung on to the belief that Jeremy would change and my marriage would be restored. Unfortunately, that fallacy is what had led to my complete denial of my circumstances. I started to become very angry with Jeremy. We could hardly be in the same room before a fight would erupt. In my mind, he was to blame for every horrible situation we were facing, and I was determined to punish him for it.

I was in the heart of the trial. And I was doing anything but rejoicing. I was determined that Jeremy had to be punished for what he'd done. I refused to let him forget what he'd done to me. The truth of the matter was that this was no longer about Jeremy. Not at all. It became completely about me. But I couldn't deal with the harsh reality of introspection and self-analysis. I was too prideful to admit that although Jeremy had started the ball rolling with his initial betrayal, God had plans for me too. This wasn't about Jeremy "having to learn his lesson" and all I had to do was just stand by and watch. No, God had a plan for me in this as well. And was I in for the ride of my life!

2. Forgiving the Unforgivable

What comes to mind when you think of the word *forgiveness*? No doubt, the answer is vastly different for each of us as we consider our life experiences. For some, it is something we have done, an act that has freed us from the bondage of anger, bitterness, and rage. For others, it is something that we hope to do, but we can't bring ourselves to release that person from the pain they have caused us. Yet for others still, it is something they can't imagine doing, as the pain caused by that person is too great to release. No matter which scenario describes your situation, forgiveness is a choice and one that is available to all, no matter the circumstances.

Why is forgiveness necessary and essential for our emotional and spiritual well-being and health? How does holding on to anger, resentment, and rage affect our lives? Why do we resist releasing those who have hurt us? Why should we "give a pass" to people who have affected our lives so terribly and profoundly? How do we forgive those who continue to hurt us, maybe on a daily or weekly basis?

You may be saying, "I can't do this" or "I am not strong enough to do this." Others may say, "I have no desire to do this" or "You don't know how So-and-So has hurt me and continues to hurt me." My heart goes out to all who have been hurt, victimized, neglected, traumatized, and abandoned. I am truly sorry for your pain, your loss, and the struggle you are enduring at the hands of another. But there is no pain, loss, or desperation too great for God to heal. "Jesus replied, 'I am the bread of life. No one who comes to me will ever be hungry again. Those who believe in me will never thirst'" (John 6:35). Jesus promises that all of your needs, physical, emotional, and spiritual, will be met when you surrender your life to Him. But you have to surrender. You have to be willing to lay your pain at the foot of the cross.

I could produce a wonderful array of biblical reasons why we are called to forgive our offenders. But the most compelling reason of all is that Jesus forgave His. "Father, forgive them for they know not what they do" (Luke 23:34). Now Jesus endured the most horrific, brutal, excruciating death one could possibly imagine. There is nothing we could possibly go through on this earth that would compare to what He *willingly* endured. I emphasize that because that makes Jesus even more amazing to me. Now, admittedly, most of us are kicking and screaming at onset of the slightest discomfort. We feverishly find a way to avoid any pain, frustration, or struggle. Not Jesus. He knew the Father had a plan for Him, and He submitted to that plan.

What did Jesus really experience? It's one thing to know in your head that Jesus died on the cross. We can hear that, but it really lacks emotional impact for most. Anyone who has seen or witnessed a tragedy can tell you how horrific and traumatic it is. But for those of us who hear it on the news or read it in the newspaper, it is simply the news of the day. Death by crucifixion is the cruelest and most torturous death any human being can endure. There have been many movies depicting the life and death of Jesus. One of my favorites is *Son of God*. I highly recommend it to all who want to learn more about Jesus, the beauty of His life, and the agony of His death.

THE POWER OF FORGIVENESS

If Jesus Christ, who was brutalized for our sins, asked for forgiveness for *us*, tell me again why you are unable to forgive. In fact, I encourage you to make a list right now of why you will not offer forgiveness. List all of the reasons you believe you are justified for not forgiving your offender. Take some time to complete this exercise. Then lay that list next to the picture of Jesus hanging on the cross. For you. For me. How does your list compare to that?

Another compelling reason to forgive is that we are commanded to forgive. The concept of forgiveness is mentioned over one hundred times in the Bible. That tells me that forgiveness is something God wants us not only to understand but also to *do*. And I'm so thankful that He knows our stubborn hearts and addresses the topic that many times. He obviously knows that forgiveness is something most of us will struggle with intensely. We serve a God who understands our challenges and is faithful to make a way for us to obey Him.

Now, I'm a firm believer in this whole forgiveness thing. At least I was until my husband decided to run our marriage into the ditch. That kind of changed things a bit for me. Now all those messy feelings like anger, bitterness, rage, hurt, and sadness kept getting in the way of my destination of forgiveness. And I seemed to be okay when he wasn't around or I didn't think about him. Unfortunately, those were two scenarios that I could not avoid. On top of it, I was living with the consequences of his sin daily. I was a single mother, breadwinner, and homemaker and had been completely abandoned by him. Every trial I faced was a brutal reminder of what he'd done to me and how none of this would have been this way if he had only read the book on being a decent husband. He didn't particularly care for reading. Not even the CliffsNotes.

I was fully committed to serving and honoring God despite these circumstances. And I was determined to have God be glorified in this mess. I knew that if that was going to happen, it would have to be with me. Why? Because I'm the only one I can control. For the longest time I believed that God was going to be glorified through the restoration of my marriage. When that didn't happen, I knew there was a beautiful message buried under all of the rubble. And after tireless digging and excavating, I found it. The message God had for me was that you can be triumphant even in the worst of battles. That you can emerge stronger and healthier than you could have been in any other way. In fact, what had happened in my marriage *had* to happen. It was *essential* to my growth. This wasn't an earthly battle at all. Yes, it involved my husband and me, but the battle was truly a spiritual one. And God was the commander in charge. Nothing happened outside of His control or His watch. He knew exactly what was taking place and how each piece of the puzzle was going to fall.

This realization was key to my being able to forgive Jeremy. Without understanding the purpose of the pain, you can't allow it and accept it as necessary. God allowed that pain in my life to help me deal with issues from my past, my dependency on others instead of Him, and my selfishness, among many, many other things. When I look back to the person I was prior to that happening to me, I wouldn't trade it for the world. Now, when I say that, most people look at me like I have two heads. Clearly this is the verbiage of a crazy person. But I stand behind the truth of that statement. I wouldn't trade one tear, one lonely night, or one horrible feeling of abandonment for the treasure that lay at the end of that journey. Without pain and adversity, there is no healing and growth. It is that simple. Allow that realization to sink in. And allow it to transform your heart and mind.

That first fateful night that Jeremy didn't come home, God planted a seed. The digging of the soil was horribly painful. And He kept digging deeper and deeper with each passing year, with each hurt that ripped at my heart. But He knew the seed had to be embedded deep within the ground. And He dug and dug for what seemed like forever. But at some point along my journey, He dropped the seed. Then He started filling in the gaping hole that remained. All of the dirt He had dug out was all the awful parts of Dana that had to go. He shoveled out anger, pride, selfishness, and dependence.

As He began to fill in the hole, He replaced Dana with the attributes of His beautiful Son, Jesus. Patience, kindness, tenderheartedness, love, selflessness, mercy, and grace began to define my character. I started caring less about me and more about others. I learned what real love was for the first time in my life. You see, before this, the only love I knew was love of self. I understood about dying to myself so Christ could live in me.

The Bible says: "If I could speak all the languages of earth and of angels, but didn't love others, I would only be a noisy gong or a clanging cymbal. If I had the gift of prophecy, and if I understood all of God's secret plans and possessed all knowledge, and if I had such faith that I could move mountains, but didn't love others, I would be nothing. If I gave everything I have to the poor and even sacrificed my body, I could boast about it, but if I didn't love others, I would have gained nothing" (1 Corinthians 14:9 NLT).

This is one of the most powerful verses in scripture to me. Faith to move mountains, giving everything to the poor—most would say that is pretty amazing faith. But what does this passage really say? Without *love*, none of that means anything. It is crucial that we understand the love that God commands us to have for everyone. Loving is not an option. It is not something we decide to do once the other person does what we expect them to do. God does not say to love only those who love you. He doesn't say to love only the ones who deserve it. No, His Word says to love. Plain and simple. We must learn to do this. But how and where do we start?

MOUNTAIN-MOVING LOVE

For the most part, it is easy to love the people whom we get along with, especially the ones we choose to be in our life. The struggle comes when someone hurts us, betrays us, lies to us, cheats on us, steals from us, abandons us. Most of us could continue to add many other offenses to this list. We are left with sorrow, pain, anger, resentment, and bitterness. How in the world do we forgive when such incredibly powerful negative emotions have center stage in our hearts and minds? Now, anyone who has felt at least one of these emotions knows how overpowering and dominating these feelings can be. They are like a fire. As we continue to feed them, they grow more intense as time goes on. Pretty soon, we have a raging inferno with no water in sight to exhaust the flames. The problem is, the ones consumed in the end are us. This kind of fire leads to a slow, painful, torturous death. While the one we feel the emotions toward isn't giving us a second thought. Think about that. We are committing suicide with unforgiveness. What intelligent, somewhat rational person would choose such lunacy? That would be most of us—until we meet Jesus.

There are so many things I love about Jesus. But one of my absolute favorites is His incredible compassion and love for sinners. What is a sinner? Who is a sinner? The harsh reality is we *all* are sinners. "For everyone has sinned; we all fall short of God's glorious standard" (Romans 3:23 NLT). Notice the verse says *everyone*, not *some* of us. Everyone includes everyone, and that would be you and me. Why is it that we like to qualify or assign severity to the sins of others? We assume that murder is worse than theft, that adultery is worse than lying. I challenge anyone to find one verse in scripture that confirms this premise. It's just not there. Sin is sin, plain and simple. Regardless of the offense, in God's eyes, it's all the same.

So often we struggle not so much with the sin committed but with the consequences that follow. For example, the sins of Jeremy left many brutal consequences for me and my parents. And the aftereffects of these consequences will be felt for years to come. Some will probably never subside. Without the power of Christ in us, we can easily become bitter as each reminder of the sin emerges in our lives. The financial pressures, the diminished bank accounts, dreams unrealized, relationships strained. This list is clearly not exhaustive. The harsh reality is that sin has lasting effects. Just like a prism reflects different colors as you hold it at different angles in the light, the same is true for an offense committed against you.

In my case, there are many reasons I could be angry with Jeremy and continue to blame him for my current situation. And those reasons would be valid and true. As I continue along that trail of thought, my emotions quickly follow. I experience feelings of anger, bitterness, sadness, and so forth. And these feelings intensify the longer I think about the offense. Now, let's turn the prism slightly as we hold it up to the light. There are different colors reflected. As I behold this side of the prism, I see my situation through the Word of God. I see that nothing happened to me that was outside of God's control and knowledge. I see that He works all things for good for those who love Him. I see that He made beauty from ashes in that I am a stronger woman. But most importantly, my relationship with the Lord has grown much deeper as I learned to rely totally on Him in my pain. Instead of focusing on myself and what was done to *me*, I focus on God and what *He* intended to do in the battle. He is sovereign and in control. If you really believe that, your pain is no longer about the person who caused it. It's about God and His plan. That realization makes all the difference.

PRAYER IN THE ASHES

Now, prior to all of this happening, I had a weak relationship with God. I went to church every Sunday, and Jeremy and I hosted a small group in our home once, but that was about all the effort I exerted. And I really didn't think much of His absence in my life on a grander scale. I know that God wanted to be Lord of my life and was not going to let me continue without Him at the helm. He allowed my life circumstances to unfold such that I would walk straight into the arms of His Son. And that I did. Now this didn't happen overnight. It was a long, painful, grueling process. But God never takes us to a place where He doesn't provide for our every need at the time.

Almost as soon as I moved to Pittsburgh, I found a church and started going weekly. I joined a women's Bible study and a group for moms with young children. Instantly I met some amazing women there, some of whom have turned out to be my closest friends. God knew that my life was about to take a nosedive, and He made sure I had support and encouragement, that I had friends to call upon, even though I wasn't ready to reveal the truth of my life to them at that time. Some of these friends knew that Jeremy and I were strained, and they offered to help as they could. God will never lead you to a place where He doesn't provide for your needs. He knew that I would need friends to talk to and shoulders to cry on. I am so thankful that He cares so much about every single detail of our lives.

Now at the time I assumed this whole ordeal was just going to blow over. I believe that is what got me through in the beginning. When I started to realize that wasn't going to happen, I had to look somewhere else for comfort and solace. That is when I started to seek God in a way I never had before. I began reading the Bible and praying. I developed close friendships with others who love the Lord, who were able to pray for me and my situation. But, most importantly, they were there to offer godly counsel and wisdom. And I knew they were the hands and feet of Christ in my life. I don't know where I would have been without them. God revealed His amazing and tender love for me by blessing me with these individuals. Never overlook one person whom God has placed in your life.

They just may be the angels sent by God to lead, help, support, encourage, or minister to you.

One of the most amazing things that happened in the aftermath of my marital disaster was that I really learned to pray and talk to God. He showed me what it was like to really have a relationship with Him. When all was ripped away, I was left in the most vulnerable but opportunistic place in my life. As I lay in a heap on the floor, I had nowhere to look but up. And that's when I saw His face. And my prayer life was never the same.

I wish I could say that this journey of healing and growth was a short uphill jaunt. But, in reality, it has taken me years to reach the plateau of wisdom, knowledge, and understanding. Today, Jeremy and I share a good relationship. I made a decision in my heart to love the unlovable, to be the hands and feet of Christ to a broken man, to love beyond myself and beyond what seems rational. God began an incredible work in me many years ago to bring me to the place of demonstrating mercy and grace. The most powerful motivation for me was truly understanding what Jesus was saying in Matthew 6:14: "If you forgive those who sin against you, your heavenly Father will forgive you. But if you refuse to forgive others, your Father will not forgive your sins." But Jesus didn't stop there. He knew our stubborn hearts would need reminding of this command. He said in Mark 11:25, "But when you are praying first forgive anyone you are holding a grudge against, so that your Father in heaven will forgive your sins, too."

The key to my freedom and redemption from emotional pain and bondage was allowing this command to take root in my heart. In dying to myself and my emotions, the power of Christ was released in me to love in a way that would truly bring healing to Jeremy. God slowly began replacing my thoughts with His. He began changing my heart to more closely resemble the heart of His Son. My pain no longer mattered. But giving God all the glory became my passion. It became the desire of my heart that my pain be utilized as a lighthouse to all who are suffering, because so many are suffering every day with pain that at times feels unbearable, pain that seems unescapable, pain that debilitates and profoundly affects every area of their lives. But God did not intend for us to carry this pain and emotional torment on our own. He made a way for us to be set free. And Jesus is that Way.

The apostle Paul said the following in 2 Timothy 2:18–13:

> Always remember that Jesus Christ, a descendent of King David, was raised from the dead. This is the Good News I preach. And because I preach this Good News, I am suffering and have been chained like a criminal. But the word of God cannot be chained. So I am willing to endure anything if it will bring salvation and eternal glory in Christ Jesus to those God has chosen. This is a trustworthy saying: If we die with him, we will also live with him. If we endure hardship, we will reign with him. If we deny him, he will deny us. If we are unfaithful, he remains faithful, for he cannot deny who he is.

Paul profoundly said, "I am willing to endure anything." Anything! Oftentimes when we pray or read scripture, we ask God to do these things in our lives. But do we truly understand what we are asking? When I told Jesus I would endure anything, I wasn't planning on having the "anything" happen in my life. Yes, Lord, I will endure anything, but please allow blessings and good things to happen to me. But that is not always God's way. Brokenness, pain, and hardship are the refining ways that God draws us closer to Him. Until we understand that, we will remain trapped in the cycle of despair, self-pity, and hopelessness.

The key to overcoming any difficulty, pain, trauma, loss, heartbreak, or disaster is understanding that God is using it all for our good. "To all who mourn in Israel, he will give a crown of beauty for ashes, a joyous blessing instead of mourning, festive praise instead of despair. In their righteousness, they will be like great oaks that the Lord has planted for his own glory" (Isaiah 61:3). This has become one of my favorite verses, and it is one that helped me overcome such painful periods in my life. Let's take a closer look at each promise, because such glorious hope is found in each one.

"To all who mourn in Israel, he will give a crown of beauty for ashes." In my work as a Clinical Psychologist, I have been blessed with the privilege of working with patients who are grieving the loss of loved ones. I had never walked that road myself, but God had equipped me to assist Him in bringing peace and hope in such heart-wrenching times. There is something about grief that debilitates us to the very core. There are no words to capture the profound pain, sorrow, and isolation that the loss of loved ones produces. There is an agony that, at times, feels unquenchable. It can feel unrelenting and endless. The pain, incredibly deep, can feel as if nothing on earth can extinguish it. And right there is where our healing begins.

Nothing on earth will quench it. Nothing on earth will comfort. And left to our own devices, we will spin out of control with questions of why, feelings of anger at the loss, doubts about the goodness of God, and the belief that our life has lost its purpose. The intensity of these emotions must be fought on our knees. Without divine comfort, we are destined to dwell in the chamber of despair and sadness.

DEATH BRINGS LIFE

On May 2, 2015, I was preparing to meet my boyfriend at Seven Springs for the evening. I was so looking forward to this trip and having a night away. Life was good, everything was peaceful, and I was well aware of the many blessings and beautiful things in my life. I had a wonderful, godly boyfriend, beautiful children, wonderful parents, and a job that I loved and was honored to do. I was blessed with such amazing friendships, and I could hardly contain my gratitude to God for all I had been given. My children were spending the evening with my parents, and we made the short five-minute commute to their home. When we pulled in their driveway, my parents were outside waiting for us. My life imploded in the one minute that followed my getting out of the car.

My father approached me and asked if I had talked to my brother. Panic struck immediately. I cannot explain why, but I knew something was amiss. He told me that he had left several messages for him and that his phone calls were not returned. My brother lived in San Diego, so our access to him was limited. I told my father that I would attempt to call Michael on my way to Seven Springs. As I drove away, a wave of fear and panic washed over me. Horrific thoughts of his death tortured me. Fear terrorized me.

That drive to Champion, Pennsylvania, was one of the longest of my life. I must have looked like a crazy person to my fellow drivers on the highway. Tears streamed down my face as I hit the steering wheel, screaming "No!" to God. Something dep within me knew I would never see my brother again. And this cut me to the very core of my being. Moments would come over me where I would tell myself that I was being ridiculous and that I knew nothing for sure. But of this I could not convince myself. For I knew in my soul that my brother was gone. And the sorrow and pain that engulfed me was only the beginning of my nightmare.

As soon as I arrived, I rushed to my boyfriend, hugging him so tight that I nearly choked him. He didn't know why I was behaving this way, but he just held me. After I explained what had happened at my parents' home, he attempted to console me and tell me everything was going to be okay. I became angry with him as I broke free from his arms. I told him that he didn't understand and that I just knew something was wrong. He invited me to sit with him and encouraged me to enjoy our evening. But the concept of enjoyment was the farthest thing from my mind. I was on a mission, a horrific, gut-wrenching mission that altered the course of my life forever.

I knew my only help would come from the San Diego Police Department. As I sat on hold for what seemed like days, my heart raced as I fought back tears. I walked outside to the deck and sat on the ground in the sunlight. I lifted my head to allow the warm sun to radiate over me. But I felt nothing. I was numb as horrible thoughts raced through my mind. Once the dispatcher came on the line, I began speaking feverishly. I then had to answer what seemed like a litany of questions that only served to anger and frustrate me. I just wanted to scream, *Quit wasting my time and find my brother!* Obviously, she didn't read my mind as this interrogation continued.

I then heard an answer that infuriated me to the very core. I was told that the police could do nothing because my brother had no significant history that would lead them to suspect a problem. I pleaded with the dispatcher, begging her with a passion deeper than I had ever experienced. I wanted to scream, *Don't you realize we are talking about my best friend? One of the most important people in the world to me? How dare you tell me you can't check on him!* But, I said none of those things. I begged her to please send someone anyway. She said the officer would try to make it over there. And with that, the call ended. And there I sat, motionless, speechless, and without my even knowing I was being changed forever.

Like a zombie I walked back inside. My boyfriend was in the kitchen cooking, as he usually did, listening to music through his headphones. He shot me a smile, but his countenance changed immediately when he studied my face. As he turned off his music, he asked me what was wrong. I can't remember a single word I said, but I'm sure it sounded like *Something is wrong with my brother.* His attempt at reassurance fell on deaf ears again. He encouraged me to get myself ready so we could enjoy a nice dinner out. I knew that what he was suggesting was best, so I pulled myself together, and we headed out.

I have not one single memory of that dinner or that evening. I experienced what I can only describe as a panic deep in my soul, desperate for a phone call, an answer, anything to bring an end to the mystery of my brother's whereabouts. Memories of my sweet brother flooded my mind. My brother and I shared a closeness and friendship that most people never experience in a lifetime. He and I weren't just siblings, we were best friends. We were a huge part of each other's lives. We shared the same friends, lived together in adulthood in California, and talked to each other about anything. I was blessed to have many friends, but there was none like him. He was the one person who carried my secrets, knew my fears, listened to me without ever a word of complaint or frustration, and was my biggest fan and cheerleader. When the world would let me down, I always knew my brother would be there to lift me up. He would always say, "You're Dane! Everything will be okay!" His faith and confidence in me, no matter how undeserving I felt of it, always carried me through and allowed me to hold my head high.

We had a loyalty to each other that, after his death, others told me they envied and admired. We were tied together at the very core of our beings, and I couldn't ever imagine life without him.

When I awoke the next day, it was before the sunrise. I was tortured with the pain of not knowing where my brother was and that the San Diego police were not understanding the gravity of this situation. I grabbed my phone and placed another call to them. Like a bull in a china shop, I was relentless when I got them on the phone. It was explained to me that they hadn't gone to his home the night before because they didn't have enough reason to do so. I begged and pleaded for them to go to his apartment, telling them I knew something wasn't right. This time, the dispatcher told me they would send someone and that they would call me when they got there. I was thankful and relieved for that information but, at the same time, filled with complete dread.

A few hours later, a police offer called me asking for my brother's apartment manager's phone number, explaining that they needed access to the building. I feverishly gathered this information as I worked overtime to keep my voice from shaking and to keep my head clear. This was it. They were outside the building, and I was about to experience the longest three hours of my life.

I went through the motions of picking up my children from my parents' house and explaining to my parents that I had called the police. Like a dam holding back the raging waters, I wanted to protect my parents from what I knew in my soul lay ahead. I masked my terror and fear as I said goodbye to them and drove off. I knew I couldn't go home, so I took my children to Rollerblade at the Murrysville Sportzone. I laced up their skates, and off they went. I paced the arena feverishly with an anguish in the core of my soul. My phone, glued to my side, lay silent as I waited for what seemed like days for it to ring. I heard my children laughing and playing, but I felt like I was in another world. I was caught between two realities, my beautiful life and the hell that I was living as I waited.

The phone's ringing startled me out of my stupor. I quickly answered it. What followed was what I can only describe as the most horrific nightmare I could ever experience. The San Diego coroner introduced herself and said the words that ripped my whole world apart. Michael had been found dead upon search of his apartment. I dropped the phone and fell to the floor, my body shaking uncontrollably. As I screamed "No!" I lay in a heap on that arena floor, sobbing uncontrollably. As I picked up that phone, of which I wanted no part, I heard the phrases *gunshot wound* and *dead for days*. I have no recollection of what else she said to me. My mind was crippled, unable to process anything other than that my brother was dead and my life had just ended. I remember calling my mother, telling her what no child should have to tell their parents: "He's dead."

Death by suicide. Questions from police followed: "Did he own a gun?" "Was he left-handed?" "Did he have psychological issues?" Hours of questions from police were followed by a graphic description of what they found at his apartment. The very same phone that I had waited desperately to ring was one I wanted to throw off the highest cliff. That phone had become the tool that hijacked my life and destroyed my world.

The days that followed are all a blur to me now. The shock and terror I felt are beyond the scope of words or description. I have very little memory of the days and weeks that followed the news of my brother's death. It was a desperate fight every day to keep living a life that I couldn't imagine without him in it. The emotions that flooded me are the most intense I have ever experienced. For the first time in my life, I was in an inferno that blazed higher and higher without any water to extinguish its flames. Completely overtaken, I fell prey to the blaze as I felt I was slowly losing my mind.

As the days turned to weeks, my only consolation came from friends and family as they would write and email tributes to my brother and me about the beauty of our relationship. My brother was so deeply loved and admired, and their words offered me comfort as the sun continued to rise each new day. I would fight back feelings of anger, hopelessness, guilt, and regret. These turned out to be the most profound, transforming days of my life. Prayer become my lifeline—my only source of sanity. I was never the same after losing my brother. God refined me, chiseled me, excavated me, and revealed Himself to me with such power that couldn't have been done any other way. That transformation can only be explained as being purified in the fire. I wasn't burned at all; in fact, I was expertly molded and shaped into a woman of strength, long-suffering, and selfless love.

Prayer is defined as a solemn request for help or expression of thanks addressed to God. There are over seven thousand promises God makes to us in the Bible. A promise is a declaration that one will do something specified. So as we make our requests and petitions known to God, His Word says that He will always respond. It is beyond comprehension that the God of the universe not only hears us but also answers us! Sadly, far too many of us don't realize that, let alone talk to God on a daily basis. There are so many reasons people don't pray with power as they should. I believe one of the biggest reasons is a failure to understand the love of God and His heart of mercy and kindness toward them, that He longs for a relationship with you and is waiting for you to pour your heart, fears, and desires out to Him. God says in His Word, "You will seek me and find me when you seek me with all your heart" (Jeremiah 29:13).

If I asked you what the desire of your heart is at this moment, what would you say? What we desire reveals a great deal about our priorities and values. For many the answer would be money, a better job, a spouse, children, a vacation home. The list is endless. In and of themselves, these things are not inherently bad. But when they become the driving force of our lives, we will end up depleted, tired, unfulfilled, and wondering why we "can't just be happy." We've all heard the saying "Money can't buy happiness." And most would agree. Perhaps being "happy" is the wrong goal. What if our goal was to have peace and joy in our lives? Now that goal would change everything!

If there is one thing most of us share in common, it's that we all have problems and we want them solved immediately. I have never met anyone who has reported delight or satisfaction with the problems they face. As a culture we seek many ways to solve, manipulate, alleviate, or eliminate the problems we face. We complain about them, run from them, deny them, self-medicate them, or blame them on someone else—anything to ease the pain they bring and avoid the emotional ramifications that follow. We have come to view problems as terrible things that happen to us. I am suggesting that problems, seen from another perspective, are actually God's promises to us.

Perspective in life is everything. As a psychologist, I have found that most people present with a negative view of the problems they face. The problems and their damaging effects on their lives are clearly articulated in session. There is then the unspoken expectation that, together, we are going to make these problems disappear, that by giving them a name and analyzing the collateral damage, the person in question will be free from the pain they cause. The problem with that approach is that our problems weren't mean to be solved; they were meant to be embraced.

Embracing problems, pain, and difficulty flies in the face of what comes natural to us. We want to feel good, to enjoy a problem-free life, and to have everything just "work out." One look at scripture shows us that this is not the natural course of our life here on earth.

"That is why we never give up. Though our bodies are dying, our spirits are being renewed every day. For our present troubles are small and won't last very long. Yet they produce for us a glory that vastly outweighs them and will last forever! So don't look at the troubles we can see now rather, we fix our gaze on things that cannot be seen. For the things we see now will soon be gone, but the things we cannot see will last forever" (2 Corinthians 4:16–8).

HOW DO WE PRAY?

In an effort to problem-solve our lives, our minds spin daily with thoughts, fears, and anxieties. We worry about everything and attempt to control our future by planning out every scenario we can imagine. The problem is that this just doesn't work. So we circle the drain, hoping the next articulate plan we create will work out. Our anxiety continues to mount as our best efforts at problem-solving fail. This leads to a dangerous cycle of hopelessness and helplessness, believing that our situation will never change.

How do we go from minds that spin like tornados to being blanketed with peace amid the storm? The Bible tells us, "You keep him in perfect peace whose mind is stayed on you, because he trusts in You" (Isaiah 26:3). Where our minds are focused is what will determine our emotional state. When our minds are stayed on God, there will be peace. When they are stayed on work, our health, our fears, and our anxieties about our children, peace will elude us. There is no permanent comfort in any of those things, because they constantly change. Work will not consistently stay fruitful. We may argue with our spouses. Our children may veer off the wrong path in life, and then we encounter sleepless nights worrying about their well-being. There is a better way to live than that.

What does work is bringing our requests, fears, and worries to the Lord. Not only does He hear us, but also He is the only one who can bring lasting change and healing to our situation. We must be careful not to view the Lord as a genie to whom we make requests and wait for an answer just as we have prescribed it. Having a relationship with your Savior is paramount and should precede any prayer requests. A heart of gratitude and thanks for all He has done should fill our hearts daily. The Bible says, "Devote yourselves to prayer with an alert mind and a thankful heart" (Colossians 4:2). This is a beautiful statement on how we should pray. To be alert is to be watchful and on guard. In order to be this way, we must have wisdom that is only given us from above.

How does one become wise? We must be careful here because many of us our wise in our own eyes. This is a very dangerous position to hold. Only God knows the path, decisions, and plans for our lives. To be wise, we must seek the Lord daily, asking Him to convict us of sin and give us a repentant heart, and then we must surrender our lives and decisions to Him. When we ask the Holy Spirit to control our lives, He will use our anxieties as a signal that a choice or decision is not in our best interests. As you become more attuned to God's voice, anxiety will drive you to prayer and lead you to wait on the Lord until He gives you peace in a situation.

Any decision made while experiencing anxiety should be a major red flag that you are headed down a treacherous path. Stop dead in your tracks and make your request to the Lord. As you learn to wait on Him, He will show you the path to walk.

The first step is to create a time in your day that is dedicated to the Lord. Whether this is the morning hours before you start your day, during your free time at lunch, or in the evening before bed, you must be intentional about spending time with God. Be purposeful in planning this time daily. This is a discipline that may take some time. But find your favorite quiet place in your home and practice sitting with your journal and Bible. As you devote your time to the Lord, He will bless you with peace that passes all understanding. Over time, you will begin to crave these moments and make them the top priority of your day. Your life will change radically, and quickly, if you begin this practice.

Begin by thanking God for all He has done. The beauty of this journal is that you will be able to look back at how God has answered your prayers. This is incredibly powerful in reminding you of God's faithfulness to you. Many times we see how God has answered prayer, but then the next trial hits us in life and we quickly revert to fear, doubt, and worry. Prayer and a record of God's faithfulness will become your armor in defending against this inclination. Offer your praise to the Lord for all He has done, for all He has provided, and for His loving care in your life. Praise Him in the situations you don't understand, believing that He has a greater plan and fully intends to bless you and increase your faith in Him.

Ask God to reveal to you any secret or hidden sin. Oftentimes our minds have been blinded to these patterns of reacting or behaving. Often originating in childhood, these patterns can be pervasive and are some of our worst coping mechanisms. As God reveals these to you, write about them in your journal and ask Him to remove them from your life. These will also serve as evidence of God's answered prayers in your life.

This prayer journal is designed to help you begin to pray for God's intervention in all areas of your life. In my professional experience, people will admit to praying, but in general terms. Prayers such as "Give me peace," "Help me," and "Guide me" are common pleas. However, God wants us to ask for far more than that. Can you imagine asking your spouse to help you but not also mentioning how he or she can assist? It is unlikely your request will be granted if your spouse doesn't know what you need. Now we know God knows our hearts and thoughts. What you are asking for help with is not a mystery to Him. But He longs for your trust and faith in Him to answer exactly what you ask in prayer. When you pray specifically, God is ultimately glorified for His faithfulness and provision.

You will be encouraged through your journey of prayer to pray specifically. This may be uncomfortable for you at first. And you may seriously question if God will really answer you. But if you pray God's Word and seek Him with all your heart, He will surely answer you. This is a guarantee. What is the secret of praying specifically? Don't just ask God, "Bless my relationships." Pray for each person in your life individually. If you know they are going through something difficult, ask God to give them wisdom. If you are concerned about your finances, ask God to give you His heart for your spending. Ask Him to place a guard on your finances so that you will only spend money according to His will. As you pray this, the Holy Spirit will be swift to fill you with conviction as you consider or begin a purchase outside of God's will.

THE POWER OF GOD'S WORD

The true power of this prayer journey becomes evident as you add scripture to your prayers. When you pray God's Word, He answers 100 percent of the time. So spend time in His Word. See what He has to say about the situation you are praying about. If you are praying about a future decision and desperately covet God's direction, write Proverbs 5–6 after your prayer request; "Trust in the Lord with all your heart; do not depend on your own understanding. Seek his will in all you do, and he will show you which path to take." In my professional work, many have expressed that they don't know the Bible well enough to do this. Your Bible should have a concordance in the back pages where each topic is listed by category. If you are seeking to learn God's will or His promises, go to that section, and scripture references will be provided. Spend time reading those. The Holy Spirit will lead you to the scripture to pray relating to your request. This practice will allow you to grow in the knowledge of God's Word and lead you to turn to it quickly as your armor and shield in times of trouble. Write these prayers on index cards and place them where you will see them often during the day. This discipline goes a long way toward planting God's Word in your heart and giving you a defense against any doubt or fear.

If, for example, your children struggle with disobedience and rebellion, your prayer may look like this: "Lord, thank You for allowing my children to have submissive, humble hearts that seek to honor and obey You in word and action." If you struggle with anger and often have a harsh critical tongue, ask the Lord to place a guard on your tongue and only allow words that edify others and build them up.

How can we put all that we have learned thus far into practice? In the heat of our swirling, intense emotions, how do we break the cycle and refocus our minds? How do we stop the madness? I found that the acronym STOP—silence, transform, opportunity, and praise—works beautifully to metamorphose my thinking. Simply put, we must stop the cycle and begin a new way of thinking and understanding whatever it is we are going through. I believe there is an earthly perspective, one we see so clearly like a brick wall that we can't imagine getting through. And then there is the heavenly perspective. The earthly perspective seems so obvious to us. We see the trial, hardship, hurt, pain, anger, and despair of a situation. There are tangible facts and pieces of evidence that point to the way we are feeling and interpreting a situation. The heavenly perspective requires a higher level of thinking and the guidance of the Holy Spirit to ascertain. The heavenly perspective is what God is doing in and through whatever we are facing. Focusing on this will be the key to transformation, freedom, and personal growth.

Silence

In the heat of the chaos within our minds the most important thing we can do is stop. As is so with any crisis, it is imperative that we gain control of the situation and process with clarity the best plan of action. "Be still and know that I am God" (Psalm 46:10)—such a simple yet powerful command God gives us in His Word. Silencing our minds allows us to regroup, process our thoughts, identify our fears, and turn our eyes toward God. In this moment we petition Him, asking for clarity, wisdom, and direction. We must admit that we are not capable of making sound, wise decisions on our own strength.

In this moment of silence, we identify what has our emotions and thoughts racing. Typically, fear is the culprit that keeps us enslaved to this way of thinking. What are we afraid of? What do we fear we cannot deal with or overcome? What has us angry or bitter? Label it, call it out. Write it down. And if we are honest, we admit that this fear or worry continues to return and invade our minds like a pesky fly that won't go away no matter how often we swat. The only goal in this phase is to bring to light whatever it is that has your mind and thoughts in chains.

Transform

When something is transformed, it is changed, morphed, elevated to a higher, more functional status. Our thoughts, which are dictated and tainted by emotions, must be transformed so we can see our situation through God's perspective. "Don't copy the behavior and customs of this world, but let God transform you into a new person by changing the way you think. Then you will learn to know God's will for you, which is good and pleasing and perfect" (Romans 12:2).

It is in this stage that we challenge our thoughts and fears. This is where the power of this prayer journal begins. Under each category for prayer, write a petition to the Lord. Define the fear, emotion, stronghold, or habit in the form of prayer. If we struggle with the fear of rejection or of not being good enough, we ask God to grant us freedom from the stronghold of insecurity. The power of scripture comes in when we reference it following our prayer. "For God has not given us a spirit of fear and timidity, but of power, love, and self-discipline" (2 Timothy 1:7).

Now that is praying with power! As you cry out to God and ask Him to transform your fears, He will answer! God will bless your faith and your trust in Him not only as you pray that prayer, but also as you trust Him to respond and answer. You will see your life transformed in a mighty way. If you struggle with crippling fear regarding the poor choices of your children, petition the Lord on their behalf. Ask God to guard their minds and hearts from evil and set them on the path of righteous living. "Always be joyful. Never stop praying. Be thankful in all circumstances, for this is God's will for you who belong to Christ Jesus" (1 Thessalonians 5:16–17).

If we mourn, are angry, or suffer perpetual sadness over the death of a loved one, it is only God's healing hand that can rescue us from this blanket of darkness and despair. Write your prayer to the Lord, asking for comfort and peace. You must be willing to see the person's death from His perspective. With our earthly eyes, the loss will always be seen as devastating, and we will be stuck in a pattern of reliving memories and struggling with the injustice of the person's death. We must trust in the saving power of God to heal our hearts and make us stronger through what he have endured. Such prayers as "Weeping may last through the night, but joy comes in the morning" (Psalm 30:5), "I will comfort those who mourn, bringing words of praise to their lips" (Psalm 57:18–19), and "You keep track of all my sorrows. You have collected all my tears in your bottle. You have recorded each one in your book" (Psalm 56:8) are helpful here.

Petition the Lord and pray those scriptures with incredible faith and trust, knowing that God will answer you and blanket you with His comfort and peace. Not only will He provide the comfort you request, but also He will strengthen you and enable you to comfort others who are mourning. "He comforts us in all our troubles so that we can comfort others. When they are troubled, we will be able to give them the same comfort God has given us. For the more we suffer for Christ, the more God will shower us with his comfort through Christ" (2 Corinthians 1:4–5).

Opportunity

As a young hockey player, my son receives a great deal of private and group instruction in the art and skill of the game of hockey. Coaches expertly guide, and whiteboards are scribbled on, as my son and the young men on his team learn the techniques of the sport. But without the precious practice time, all instruction is worthless. Jesus tells us in James 1:22, "But don't just listen to God's word. You must do what it says. Otherwise, you are only fooling yourselves." My son can listen to instruction all day long, but until he puts into practice all that he has learned, his hockey skills will remain unchanged.

Much the same is true with changing our thoughts and behaviors. Now that we have identified the thoughts and beliefs that hold us captive to the same dysfunctional way of behaving and responding, we must put into practice a new way of responding. If we are prone to angry outbursts and to retaliating with hurtful words, we must allow our minds to be transformed into a healthier way of responding. Instead of walking away, offering our partner the silent treatment, or spewing hurtful words, we stop. In the heat of the moment we acknowledge our emotions and how we are feeling. If need be, we sit silently as we allow our emotions to calm and our minds to gain clarity. As this happens, we gain greater perspective of the situation and become better able to communicate in a healthy way.

This calmness of mind allows us to communicate with the goal of resolution instead of with perceived righteousness. Instead of seeking to "win" or be right, we seek the greater good of the relationship. Our goal becomes solving the problem instead of winning the war. As you pray for your loved ones and other people in your life, God will lead you to respond to each in His way, employing mercy, grace, and a heart of understanding.

Praise

Our praise is the most powerful weapon against anything we face, any obstacle in our relationships, and any behavior that we just can't change on our own that continues to strangle us and keep us down. "Yet you are holy, enthroned on the praises of Israel" (Psalm 22:3). God inhabits the praises of His people. It is crucial that we understand the magnitude of this verse. The God of the universe is right there with you as you praise Him. It is our human tendency to focus on what is wrong, what we don't have, or what we wish we had instead of on the multitude of blessings in our lives. Praising God by speaking a word of thanks, singing or listening to worship music, or talking about His goodness with others is a way to magnify Him in your life. And this comes with the promise that He is right there with you, offering you peace, comfort, joy, and solace.

This prayer journal will be a powerful tool for praise in your life. As you record each date your prayer is answered, you will have a vivid visual for God's faithfulness in your life. As you pray for each area of your life, your growth can be seen visually in each area you commit to prayer. Be thorough, utilizing each section of prayer. Be detailed. Make your prayers very specific, and prepare to be amazed and blown away by how God responds to you. And as you look back at how He has transformed your life and the lives of those around you, thank Him for what He has done. God delights in our praise. Make praise a natural part of each day. He is faithful. Believe He can move mountains, and He will do so again and again in your life. Stand on that truth, and make praising Him as natural as breathing.

So why not embark on this new season of prayer in your life? You will be amazed, humbled, and awestruck at the relentless love of the Lord for you. The prayer journal is broken down into various areas of your life that you can commit to prayer. This will encourage you to begin the journey of daily prayer time with God. On each line, you can write the date and your prayer request. You are also encouraged to add the scriptures, God's promises, to each petition. This is where the real power lies. As each prayer is answered, you are encouraged to write the date it was answered as your reference to God's faithfulness and love for you. What God says He will do in His Word, He will do! When you have filled the pages of this book, you may use a separate journal to continue this discipline of prayer and time with God. Each journal will prove to be a vivid example of not only your journey of faith but also God's unrelenting love, mercy, and grace for you. You will be reminded that although the storms may continue to rage, God has helped you in the past and will continue to move your mountains in the future.

So, sit back, get comfy, and start praying with power!

MY PRAYER JOURNAL

Take some time to write what your hopes and expectations are as you begin this prayer journey. Do you believe God will answer? How hopeful are you for change? This is a great way to see how far you come and fully capture God's faithfulness after you begin this journey.

_____

_____

_____

_____

_____

_____

_____

_____

_____

_____

_____

_____

_____

_____

_____

_____

_____

_____

_____

_____

_____

_____

_____

_____

_____

MY FAITH

"I tell you the truth, if you had faith even as small as a mustard seed you could say to this mountain, 'Move from here to there,' and it would move. Nothing would be impossible for you" (Matthew 17:20).

_____

_____

_____

_____

_____

_____

_____

_____

_____

_____

_____

_____

_____

_____

_____

_____

_____

_____

_____

_____

_____

_____

_____

_____

_____

_____

_____

_____

TEMPTATIONS

"And God is faithful. He will not allow the temptation to be more than you can stand. When you are tempted, he will show you a way out so that you can endure" (1 Corinthians 10:13).

ADDICTIONS

"Don't participate in the darkness of wild parties and drunkenness, or in sexual promiscuity and immoral living, or in quarreling and jealousy. Instead, clothe yourself with the presence of the Lord Jesus Christ" (Romans 13:13–14).

FORGIVENESS

"If you forgive those who sin against you, your heavenly Father will forgive you. But if you refuse to forgive others, your Father will not forgive your sins" (Matthew 6:14–15).

_____

_____

_____

_____

_____

_____

_____

_____

_____

_____

_____

_____

_____

_____

_____

_____

_____

_____

_____

_____

_____

_____

_____

_____

_____

_____

PARENTS

"Children obey your parents because you belong to the Lord, for this is the right thing to do. 'Honor your father and mother.' This is the first commandment with a promise: If you honor your father and mother, things will go well for you, and you will have a long life on the earth'" (Ephesians 6:1–3).

CHILDREN

"Children are a gift from the Lord; they are a reward from him" (Psalm 127:3).

SPOUSE

"Give honor to marriage, and remain faithful to one another in marriage" (Hebrews 13:4).

_____

_____

_____

_____

_____

_____

_____

_____

_____

_____

_____

_____

_____

_____

_____

_____

_____

_____

_____

_____

_____

_____

_____

_____

_____

_____

_____

_____

_____

_____

_____

CAREER

"Always work enthusiastically for the Lord, for you know that nothing you do for the Lord is ever useless" (1 Corinthians 15:58).

_____

_____

_____

_____

_____

_____

_____

_____

_____

_____

_____

_____

_____

_____

_____

_____

_____

_____

_____

_____

_____

_____

_____

_____

_____

_____

_____

_____

INTEGRITY

"Joyful are people of integrity, who follow the instructions of the Lord" (Psalm 119:1).

HONESTY

"Look at those who are honest and good, for a wonderful future awaits those who love peace" (Psalm 37:37).

_____
_____
_____
_____
_____
_____
_____
_____
_____
_____
_____
_____
_____
_____
_____
_____
_____
_____
_____
_____
_____
_____
_____
_____
_____
_____
_____
_____

FINANCES

"But people who long to be rich fall into temptation and are trapped by many foolish and harmful desires that plunge them into ruin and destruction. For the love of money is the root of all kinds of evil. And some people, craving money, have wandered from the true faith and pierced themselves with many sorrows" (1 Timothy 6:9–10).

FRIENDS

"As iron sharpens iron, so a friend sharpens a friend" (Proverbs 27:17).

_____

_____

_____

_____

_____

_____

_____

_____

_____

_____

_____

_____

_____

_____

_____

_____

_____

_____

_____

_____

_____

_____

_____

_____

_____

_____

FAMILY

"But as for me and my family, we will serve the Lord" (Joshua 24:15).

_____
_____
_____
_____
_____
_____
_____
_____
_____
_____
_____
_____
_____
_____
_____
_____
_____
_____
_____
_____
_____
_____
_____
_____
_____
_____
_____
_____
_____
_____
_____
_____

WORLD

"Yet I am confident that I will see the Lord's goodness while I am in the land of the living" (Psalm 27:13).

_____

_____

_____

_____

_____

_____

_____

_____

_____

_____

_____

_____

_____

_____

_____

_____

_____

_____

_____

_____

_____

_____

_____

_____

_____

CHURCH

"Let us think of ways to motivate one another to acts of love and good works. And let us not neglect our meeting together, as some people do, but encourage one another, especially now that the day of his return is drawing near" (Hebrews 10:24–25).

JUSTICE

"Dear friends, never take revenge. Leave that to the righteous anger of God. For the Scriptures say, 'I will take revenge; I will pay them back,' says the Lord" (Romans 12:19).

HEALTH

"A cheerful look brings joy to the heart; good news makes for good health" (Proverbs 15:30).

_____

_____

_____

_____

_____

_____

_____

_____

_____

_____

_____

_____

_____

_____

_____

_____

_____

_____

_____

_____

_____

_____

_____

_____

_____

_____

_____

_____

_____

_____

HURTS

"He will cover you with his feathers. He will shelter you with his wings. His faithful promises are your armor and protection" (Psalm 91:4).

ETERNAL LIFE

"He has planted eternity in the human heart" (Ecclesiastes 2:11).

HOME

"But as for me and my house, we will serve the Lord" (Joshua 24:15).

ANGER

"And don't sin by letting anger control you. Don't let the sun go down while you are still angry for anger gives a foothold to the devil" (Ephesians 4:26).

FINDING A GODLY SPOUSE

"Don't be unequally yoked with unbelievers. How can righteousness be a partner with wickedness? How can light live with darkness" (2 Corinthians 6:14)?

MY CHILDREN'S FUTURE SPOUSES

"So again, I say, each man must love his wife as he loves himself, and the wife must respect her husband" (Ephesians 6:33).

LORD, HOW SHOULD I PRAY?

"'If you look for me wholeheartedly, you will find me. I will be found by you, says the Lord. 'I will end your captivity and restore your fortunes'" (Jeremiah 29:13).

Printed in the United States
By Bookmasters